T0314376

PRAISE FOR *PHOSPHENE*

I readied myself to read *Phosphene*. Gathered snacks, lit candles and checked in with all of my beautiful darknesses. I opened a window to let some of them out along with the energy trapped inside my incense and smoke. This werk of Brandon's is an invitation to dig deep and validate your self fully. To believe in the truth that is your breaking and your growth. Academia; take heed and catch up. This here is what a culminating experience looks like. It is work I will gladly reference. *Phosphene* is thesis, research and methods that offers us each space to get more free in its conclusion.

—SARAI BORDEAUX

Phosphene by Brandon Logans is an exploration of body and light and its haunting yet beautiful vulnerability. Interwoven between nature and danger, Brandon brilliantly challenges us as readers to think about the value of being seen and unseen, death, and the different perceptions of light; reality. On this journey, Brandon effortlessly and successfully writes layers of disorientation and sections of repetition and space on the page. Captivating and dynamic, Brandon creates a myriad of voices that describe self, one's body in relationship to the world on this earth, and survival with external limitations.

—MELISSA JONES

Brandon Andre Logans' *Phosphene* exposes the reader to a subject laboring through the realities of being, perception, & selfhood. The ominous & apathetically present light more than shines but singes through the lenses the speaker survives. *Phosphene* asks us to interrogate what is legible, visible, optical & illusory about the Others we make & Others we are. Dreamlike but more dynamic than fantastic, Logan's collection is a flickering approach to the long exposures processed under the subjugation of having a body constantly navigating inhospitable interrogation & spotlight. They write: "Splendor seizes the scene" & that spectacle is more than a show but a series of revelatory sensations.

—JZL JMZ

Phosphene reflects the best of Logans' ability to craft work that is both sharply scientific and searingly sensual. This collection is a visceral journey through questions of survival, privilege, and the ability, through it all, to "taste briefly the thrill of flying."

—MEILANI CLAY

Logans' *Phosphene* is an amalgamation of the body with earth, time, and other dimensions. An otherworldly creator of scene, Logans pulls at the fibers of our realities to transport us to a place where we must imagine new ones. *Phosphene* not only invites us on a journey serving as the antonym of stagnation, but also begs us to ask ourselves what it means to be both "curtain and perhaps the wind."

—LANDON SMITH

Brandon Logans' potently nuanced debut book, *Phosphene*, traces the jagged shape of inequity's searing light and asks, "Like this, can I survive?"

Logans stretches the limits of the page, disrupting white space. A subterranean voice presses up against the marginal boundary, straining to individuate, seeking ground against which to become figure.

This voice is housed in "a human shape in the / distance blinking in and out." Here is the body: unsettled, unsettling, falling, fallen. This body, involuntary shapeshifter, becomes, in turn, animal, elemental, geometrical, architectural. Metaphor hardens, concretized into physical form.

Logans' vivid descriptions of "this map of flesh" —permeable, fragmented, estranged—bring into focus the grotesqueries of structural violence, a violence so amorphous and diffuse as to seem invisible to those with the luxury of looking away.

The landscape of these poems is equally as destabilizing, a world constructed of mazes, mirrors, windows, and portals. Language, too, slips, splits, and spills as it veers between visceral sensorium and bureaucratic directive.

Logans refuses representational clarity; the speaker of his poems faces down the pane of legibility as an unwilling specimen who yearns to be known but not reduced: a desire in the spirit of Édouard Glissant's "right to opacity." This stance interrogates the very notion of categorization.

Light, shone directly into the eyes, disorients. Logans re-orients the reader to society's gridlocked scaffolding, its hegemonic "net," so that even ensnared, we can recognize power's blueprint and attempt to unpin its piercing gaze.

With vulnerability and vitality, Logans' urgent poems compel the reader toward the autonomy of unenlightenment through an insistently embodied avant-garde.

—CLARE LILLISTON

BLACK LAWRENCE PRESS

Executive Editor: Diane Goettel
Book Cover and Interior Design: Zoe Norvell
Cover Art: *What Have We Missed By Choosing to See No Evil?*
by Aimée M. Everett 2021

Copyright © Brandon Logans 2024

ISBN: 978-1-62557-088-8

All rights reserved. Except for brief quotations in critical articles or reviews, no part of this book may be reproduced in any manner without prior written permission from the publisher: editors@blacklawrencepress.com

In June of 2023, Black Lawrence Press welcomed numerous existing and forthcoming Nomadic Press titles to our catalogue. The book that you hold in your hand is one of the forthcoming Nomadic Press titles that we acquired.

Published 2024 by Black Lawrence Press.
Printed in the United States.

PHOSPHENE

BRANDON LOGANS

BLACK LAWRENCE PRESS

FOREWORD

Phosphene begins "I woke up," and yet there is no triumphant story about what it means to wake up, what it means to notice. At one moment, the narrator's windpipe is filled with crow feathers and they "caw with several dozen voices of a murder." In another, their mouth fills with blood.

Light in this book obscures rather than illuminates. What is real is what cannot be seen directly.

You know that moment when you close your eyes and then you put pressure on them and then you see some sort of light-based image, often something that looks like stars? That image is a phosphene. It is an image developed within the brain without light. Phosphene may be what the religious see when they see the light. And they are what people who have been deprived of light see in their darkness, the "prisoner's cinema." Astronauts see them too. As do people exposed to radiation. And those who are tripping on psychedelics.

It was J. B. H. Savigny who coined the term *phosphene*. Savigny was the surgeon on the Medusa when it was headed to Senegal to re-establish a French colony there. The captain was inexperienced, inept. He refused to see what was obvious, right in front of his eyes, basically the shore of what is now called Mauritania. After he grounded the frigate, the crew made plans to evacuate, building a raft to carry the cargo. But the grounded ship began to crack and the crew realized they had to quickly abandon it. Instead of cargo, the raft carried members of the crew. The raft was at first towed by those in lifeboats. It was slow going so those in the lifeboats cut the raft loose and it drifted on open ocean for around two weeks. Most of those on the raft died during these weeks. Some died after the eventual rescue. It was a horror story on top of the horror story that was colonialism. Savigny was one of few to survive. He had already coined the term phosphene when boarded the Medusa. But this story too, is there when this book presses on the eyes.

What is seen beneath the light, or what is right in front of our eyes but often overlooked, that's a big part of what this book is about. Some of these poems are titled a variation of "light can murder in excess." And they are only footnotes, footnotes about the difficulty of the narrator to see, about the difficulty of remembering their worth, their right to have a body, their right to inventory this body and have it matter, their right to think with it on their own terms.

There are also six sections in this book titled "Consider the Methods." Each one is an outline of circumscriptions, limitations, denials. Each of these is about how to make someone unable to speak, how to dismiss, how to deny what they know, what is right before their eyes.

"I woke up," that is how *Phosphene* begins. And it ends with a description of someone trying to speak and yet still, "suddenly you are suddenly gone."

—JULIANA SPAHR, author of
Well Then There Now and *This Connection of Everyone With Lungs*

The following is a description of slow death.

The following is a body individualized.

The following is a fragment of any picture you have seen before.

What does each day mean when you aren't sure what it means to be alive?
Who has the capacity for questions and why?

Should I assimilate into the fold for comfort?
Should I escape and bear myself, vulnerable?

The following is an attempt at leaving something behind.

The following is an altar to bring the ghosts home.

The following is me: a body, a ghost.

Dear Reader, In the following:
after the book is shut, within the bed,
against the stickiness of the rain, at the end of things,
between the margins, once this begins,

dear reader, remember to dream.

PHOSPHENE

I woke up.

Light opens out across the sky.

My feet have become fins.

I try flopping across the grass.

Sweat beads like dew along my forehead.

A crown of crows arrives along the wires above me.

A puma follows.

Four deer are next to arrive.

They encircle me and watch.

I drag myself across the lawn and hear the faint churn of water.

I hope there is a stream nearby that leads out to the sea.

The circle tightens slowly as I move.

My scales reflect brightly against the noon light.

Gasping, I feel dry as if cooking on a grill.

I know it is not too long until I will be morsels on many tongues, nutrition for the bellies of those that surround me, eventually nitrate to fertilize the earth.

I wonder why they only watch; I wonder what kind of feeling lies behind their gaze.

My nails find concrete.

I know water is not near, yet I grit my teeth and drag my body across the cement.

A rib protrudes from my side with the desperate motion of lungs trying to breathe and diffuse energy throughout my body.

An hour seems to pass by, but I can't be sure of the passage of time.

There's the waning strength in my fingertips, and the burning strain running across my arms as I press on.

The crows, puma, and deer watch.

I scream out in rage.

The sky is clear, there is not a chance of rain, and soon my body will stop.

I see a silhouette before me, a human shape in the distance blinking in and out.

I cry out, *help*.

Impatiently, a crow swoops down and nips me.

I feel blood trickle down my ear, and with that current, my consciousness slips.

Consider the Methods

1. Construct a body, emphasize its inherent qualities.
    a. One of these qualities might be that it is dangerous.
        i. If this quality is dangerous, it is easier for it to be the site of public catharsis.
            1. More clearly stated, this body must be equally vulnerable as it is dangerous.
                a. These bodies must be available to harm at all times.
            2. Order is maintained with properly regulated outlets.
    b. One of these qualities might alternatively be its innocence.
        i. Those with the most authority must always first be assumed to be innocent.
            1. This is easiest to accomplish when you construct an opposing body as dangerous.
                a. Order is maintained when there is always a body to fear.
2. When considering intrinsic attributes, be sure to make clear distinctions.
    a. It may be helpful to first begin with who is dangerous and who is innocent. It is easier then to constellate these bodies into a moral compass, attributes such as "good" or "ill-intentioned."

i. For the dangerous bodies, emphasize the static or flat qualities of their characters.

ii. The innocent bodies should be visible everywhere, stories should emphasize their capacity for change, complexity, and growth.

    1. Beauty is a side effect of these things.

        a. If you are effective in your efforts, so will love, so will stability.

Light ¹

---

1 I feel the light as layers and layers of glass. I grope along its edges, searching for gaps to slip into. I cut off pieces of my hair, trying to see if the air will catch it and that by the grace of a breeze, I could find my way out of its maze.

Light

---

2 To be hypervisible underneath light's lens is to feel as though there is nothing beneath
my skin. As if I am only a cluster of air clumps, my mouth a compass unable to find North,
my anus a facade. It's a feeling of both being full and empty at the same time, as if my
intestines were moths, blood flow sluggish sand, my hair sea glass, and my eyes mirrors.

I stare at a lot of segmented volume, occupying an expanse like a mountain range or cavern well, prairie field or sea wave, valley ditch or cliff face.

I feel compelled to contain openness in a figuration of squares; like frames.

Allocate digestible lengths and widths of material and consume them with my eye eyelid eyelash mouth apparatus.

In a serial design, successive order demands a between; a fold or partition.

For instance, imagine four walls.

Draw a slope for both shallow and deep ends.

Name it with the iris: pool.

I think I know exactly the place where I can stand unharmed, unbothered, my head just above the surface.

I wonder about the temperature of things while I am here.

Why I am not surrounded by any water or any air.

Light   ³

---

3   My feet won't seem to touch the ground, my cheeks billow with the howl of falling.
Lightly. I lack a sense of danger, heady with lightheadedness. I have learned how to fly,
like shimmer, like window pane, like reflection refracting through waves at an angle, dis-
persed. Somehow I slip, my head meets the cement curb. Teeth knock and pain blooms
into a fog, where like air, light is knocked out of me. I search for a gaze, frantically reaching
out with limbs. Rain and static bleed from a loosened skull, become a wave. Then I crash.

Foam.

I am salt breeze, sloshing, in a thinning reach.

Whispers edge back against ear shell.

I see hands, necks, and rope cling to shore.

Song wail calls wrap about my waist.

When I see blue and red lights screech down the road, my stomach tightens.

A volume of water crushes me flat.

The sails were like cloth clouds; I can still hear them in the distance crying out.

Blue tastes like jeans.

Tongue seeks a pulse through stiff fabric like a hook, teased.

Come gush down my jaw.

Uniforms, deep like full evening blues.

I look up and ask permission to breathe.

Light   ⁴

---

4   I connect mirage to tongue

Wet limbs

Spend my days kicking

Scattered

Skeletal

Sometimes gelatinous

Lodged in esophagus

Erased

Overlayed

Light

   In this insistent pressure of photons, sound becomes scrambled. My name turns on its syllables, fold and pleat into the whirr of a droll hum. Disoriented, I spill my lunch out onto the sidewalk in sloppy yellow chunks. My knees buckle, while blood puffs out of my ears.

I keep my attention on my thumb as it touched each finger in succession: pointer, middle, ring, and pinkie.

I think that maybe I am a rind with no fruit.

It is a good line, so I imagine me, writing it down.

I try to pay attention to the sidewalk in front of me.

There is the gray black road and the slate gray concrete and an end to this pavement, and this end would be a place where hopefully I could stop moving.

A place where maybe I could lie down and try to tie myself back to my bones.

The ground tilts or is it my head that tilts, and I feel a cluster of crow feathers in my windpipe.

I open my throat and caw with several dozen voices of a murder.

When I close my mouth, I notice how the blue of the sky cuts into my eyes; I look down and try to pay attention to my fingers back to my fingers back to my fingers back to fingers, back to fingers.

I think about how my fingers could be like keys or my flesh as grain for a door.

I wonder what the other side of me looks like.

People are often concerned with passing, but I know that I am first and foremost an entryway trying to pass my archway as a face and I thought maybe the span of my skin could be real as it is both stationary and tangible.

Despite this assertion, I know that there is a peephole at my throat and if you ask me I couldn't tell you what is looking out from there, or what you are looking at, or what is looking back.

Consider the Methods

1. Naturalize violence.
   a. Allow it to run like water everywhere.
2. Teach *them* not to flinch.
   a. In tandem, teach *them* not to cry.
      i. Teach *them* to hold it in, as if their bodies are a reservoir.
         1. Say it builds character.
         2. Say it is necessary for survival.

I wake up to a body falling away from the windshield.

I don't recognize my hair.

Light splits the sky.

There is this constant wound that feels similar to breathing.

Names fill my mouth, saltwater I can't seem to swallow or transmute into gold.

If I was made out of gold, would I live longer or less here?

I wake to the news, a body at my doorstep.

I wrap it in blankets.

I wash my mouth with soap and try to make room for its ghost.

I hold its head to my chest and try to sing with my heartbeat, a proper eulogy.

However, I am late to work.

I leave the body in the doorway.

When I come home, I leave my ears beneath the fridge.

I sleep and dream of planes and bodies and daffodils.

The mirror is an underworld gate and the mouth of the machine.

I wake up to a body in my kitchen.

I take two coins and place one over each eye and forget to say goodbye.

I don't have time to purchase a bouquet to mark the grave.

I'm asleep and the body is alone in a wing of a hospital, marked contagious by the band of flies encircling its temple.

I try to open the door, but it's locked.

I try to shave my finger down into a key, but the dream logic fails me and I wake to shredded skin.

My mouth fills with blood, so I must brush my teeth.

I see a letter from my landlord nailed to a body on my refrigerator.

I don't recognize my eyelashes nor my cheeks.

I go to work, hand sanitizer and knuckle bones jostling in my bag.

I can't remember what time of year it is, whether it could be so hot or too cold.

I have been sneezing for weeks, it's the only time I have to weep.

I wake up to a body, where my body should be.

I dream of a body, where my body should be.

I place a stuffed body underneath my bed in confusion, get dressed, and head for work again.

I dream again of a body shot and falling through the air.

The arms outstretched as if it could be a bird, as if it could be a plane.

Light   in excess[6]

---

6   A radiance is everywhere. Shimmering through glass, an aura of brilliance. I was told
that in light I could find beauty. In the distance, I hear the repeated phrase: *You can find
beauty here.*

Light exposes color to iris, kisses me fully and drinks from my lips. I feel exposed: the
sleek lines of my neck, the curves of my nostrils, bone, a rim of salt, the water held in
my skin, the eyelash. Dew sweat rises as crystals cascade across my forehead. Wet beads
refract, reflect.

My brain knots can be seen. The uneven row of my teeth. Flickering. I gaze into the dis-
tance. The light, like hands, reaches out and tries to hold onto my shape and volume. It
clings to the sides of skin, lingering and dragging strips back thin like hangnails to reveal
gleam of fleshblood. *You can find beauty here.*

Elation rises like punch red leaking across sky. Splendor seizes the scene. I saw body and
bounty separate in the window pane. The neck stem bending, my face, now a flower, split
open in rapture.

Light   in excess[7]

---

7   The light uses my windpipe to practice emotional breakthrough as if my bones were a pile of autumn leaves. Joy and red swells into dazzling sunset. A river bends with my neck with sign posts: Stop. Rest. If you die, take an organ please. Resurrect here. Pupils mistake evening for daybreak. I imagine myself as a wall or a well. I function as an oven or a depository. The light opens my neck and starts feasting. I am either now a molecule or unreal as I try to hold onto a notion of reality. I learned to remain calm under most instances of duress and to come when conjured. The light places a window in my back. The light forgets to remove its fingers from my mouth. I try dividing at a bend of time. The light notices movement and attempts to pin the body down. I might instead be elsewhere, with my feet singing between the clouds. Something like vapor or skin replicating itself in effort to learn how to dream.

As a song against the house:

Sinuous,

sensuous

scent

sweet

s

oft

sob

sop

saw

awl

Light   in excess[8]

---

8   I want to press my tongue across the beach to feel a real body.

Light   in excess[9]

---

9   I am unsure if I am ascending or if I am turning into a ghost. Unsure if my head is pounding, or if it's my heart, or is it someone at my door. I feel locked out from my tongue, from my nose, from my hips. I know something keeps slapping into me, it is hot. I know there is blood. I know there is me, smiling into the light and a whole hole burning through me. I gyrate my forearms back and forth against each other, move my hands over my chest and my thighs. If I sand my body down into a less intricate shape, would I become more legible? And like this, would I be considered alive?

Light in excess[10]

Light   in excess[11]

---

11   have developed a delay, as if my body is far away, and I must travel over stretches of interior space to reach it. Unruffled, I do not ask for you to stop, as you grab me inappropri- ately. Choosing instead to turn my head away. Is a short and awkward chuckle appropriate here? In the ideals of order, I imagine there are boundaries, but being clear means to allow many things to pass through. Yes, exotic materials comprise my skin, please harvest where you please. Yes, my orifices are available to be filled. Yes. Why don't you come in and poke holes into my windpipe, my skull, my heels? Yes. Yes. Yes.

Light   in excess[12]

Consider the Methods

1. First, listen.
    a. Summarize carefully and repeat.
        i. Modify where necessary to suit your needs
2. Begin your reply with, "You are overreacting."
    a. Alternatively, "You are not thinking straight."
3. Emphasize your good intentions, articulate how and where this has been a misunderstanding.
4. Do not address concerns directly.
5. Focus on your assertion, return the conversation to the primacy of your point of view.
6. When asked if communication is about a coming to terms between at least two parties, say nothing.
    a. If they persist for an answer after several minutes, repeat step 2.

I know my feet touch the earth, but I'm always struck by this feeling of being unbound.

I feel as though I am waiting to pop.

My hand reaches out to touch the wind.

I cannot seem to hold onto it, nor the light nor the sky.

Light can murder in excess[13]

---

13   Light stretches across the full length of my body. It feels like a saran wrap tight embrace or a plastic bag over my head.

Light can murder in excess[14]

---

14   I feel like I'm always open. Heart open, bleeding all over the furniture unintention-
ally. I bring my ear to the floor. My cheek smooth, the carpet rough. Contact. Eyes dilate,
exhale expelled. Inhale. I hope to expel the spell. I am flushed, feverish. I feel like a cavity,
perhaps I am just a ghost. I am told that I am dirty. All I want is to feel clean.

Light can murder in excess[15]

---

15   I want to feel like this boundary, my skin, matters. Maybe I could even be loved.
Perhaps being alive could, in fact, be nourishing. Instead of being knocked into being
knocked into being knocked into. I try to rearrange

Light can murder in excess[16]

---

16 my teeth to make a pretty white and straight smile for you. If I punch myself first will you accept my modesty or should I tear gas my eyes? Tell me what I have to do to reach the light, what must I shave off. Refine. Reify?

Light can murder in excess[17]

---

[17] My whispers are renamed mirror, as if I speak in a fog. When looked upon, I lay against the ground to remind the body is real with the concrete. By noon, I am often imperceptible except on cloudy days. When it rains, I know myself as a song against the house. A patter against the window pane, mirror on glass, frenzied rhythm, deluge refractions. When I sleep, I find myself in a bright room with too many light bulbs to count. I spin time over several daze that feel like hours or being punched in the gut or the slow pressure of hands around the windpipe. Breathing begins to feel like a wound. I want to be a beach, so I can feel acutely both the death and life buried there. I try to talk in a pattern to mimic waves or talk as if I am a motion of cleansing. When I am most alone, my sweat reminds me I am ocean. I like backstroke, because I don't have to worry about when to inhale, when to exhale. I build a home out of my hair, but my nerves constantly unloosen the foundation. If I must be a mirror against your eye, I hope that I might at least be a site for you to find yourself.

I have to remember, I am my mother's dream.

41

Light can murder in excess[18]

18 The tide pulls me outwards dragging me into its embrace, thinning my body into a line. Skin puckers, salt pickles, mouth forced ajar, bleeding. I suppose I am trying to find land, though my toes are snuggled in sand off on the shore. The horizon divides; the sky now mirror.

Consider the Methods

1. When presented with an effect, claim that there is a single cause for its origin.
    a. This may be because of skin, shape of genitalia, direction of one's attraction, etc.
2. Emphasize the relationship between this single reason and the effect. Make it so that it is a one to one equation.
    a. It is key to reduce the amount of variables.
3. Enforce firmly the idea that problems are more easily solved when isolated.
    a. Proposals to resolve singularities are more manageable.
        i.   Simple to sketch out.
        ii.   Simple to pitch.
        iii. Simple to execute.
        iv.   Simple to dismiss.

Light can murder in excess[19]

---

19   I have been wandering in this maze for many daze. My cheek has begun to slip off the side of my face, spluttering against the earth like hot rain. Dislocation describes my joints, but somehow my sight remains forward against the twists.

Light can murder in excess[20]

---

20 I walk down the streets, groping towards the azure. No one reacts. I know there is me and this disintegrating bond with myself like sunset or recalling. I often try to imagine a time outside of this time and fail. I do not feel like food, but realize I am food. My glands, fat, marrow will nourish you. I know I have value as use. Even if I end as refuse, maybe the soil might welcome me in its embrace. I attempt to smile, turning up to the sky in a whisper, "Future oh sweet future, is there place for me in your retina?"

Consider the Methods

1. Tell an individual that there are no limits to what one can do with their life.
2. Embed limitations to access in all sectors based on perceived factors.
3. If an individual fails in their goals, blame the individual for a lack of effort, a lack of will.
    a. If confronted directly, about underlying structural factors that may have influenced the individual's chances at failure, cast a spell of glamour.
        i. Say sweetly for example: No malicious acts have been done to you, this is the consequence of your own mindset. This is integral to you, based on what I can see. These inherent qualities are why you will not succeed. They may even be why you deserve to die. It's about your blood you see, on a micro level (say something about chromosomes here perhaps), we are not the same.

Light can murder in excess[21]

---

21 I try to be solved, a point that knows its place. That knows its trajectory. Sometimes though I wonder if my primary concern should be survival first. I wonder if thriving and emotional stability is really just a pubescent wet dream. No matter where I am when these questions arise, a small paper finds me. A small list to consider, font red as if in blood: 1. Do not mourn too deeply for what is already lost/what is already not available to you. 2.Try to forget. 3. Try to sleep. 4. Go back to work. 5. Time is a construct, like all things, even power, so be assured someday you will persevere, someday you could thrive.

A white woman sits on the bus waiting for her stop.

A black man comes onto the bus with bags and a speaker in his arms.

He sits down and turns on the speaker.

Luther Vandross begins to fill the air.

The music is a welcome surprise to me, a sudden wave of tenderness after a long day.

The white woman is upset by the loud noise.

Her furrowed brow gives her away despite the face mask.

The black man notices and claims that this ain't her house.

An issue of space intermingles with Luther's long notes.

The man mentions his husband; the white woman tells him to shut up.

Intersections seem to fall away at first glance.

The white woman prioritizes her womanness.

The black man prioritizes his queerness; he tells her, "I could not love you."

The white woman in her desire to reclaim the space begins to shout 99 beers on the wall.

The black man changes to a different Luther Vandross song.

He appeals to love and asks her to listen.

I drift to a memory of me and my Grandmother on the One, speeding with the sunlight as if we were stars in a movie, like we were cared for by this country, like we were alive.

Glinting, the water in the distance reflected itself within the side view mirror against my eye like a blade, it cuts into the scene agleam.

The black man turns off the music and asks the white woman, "Are you happy now?"

Did I read BLM on the white woman's shirt before I noticed the knife's edge?

She says shut up between tight teeth, while holding the blade out of his line of sight.

I, having noticed the knife, ready myself to put my body between them.

Between this black man, who has a husband, who has this tenderness, who is alive and this white woman in her Black Lives Matter tie dye shirt with her blade in hand who is ready to strike.

She, who feels threatened because of the music, perhaps because of this black man's perceived masculinity, and he who appeals for understanding, my body readies itself to place itself between them.

My body readies itself.

And then the black man stands and leaves the bus, thanking the driver.

And after two seconds, the white woman sheathes the blade.

She relaxes, while I linger on the sound of the knife's hiss as it disappears from view.

I watch as she returns the weapon into her bag.

I watch her return to "safety," muscles visibly relaxing.

After a couple more stops, she gets up to leave the bus.

The white woman turns to me while covering the letters of her shirt momentarily with her arms, she turns to me despite the door being behind her, opening her mouth to say something.

I did not hear her the first time, and she repeats herself calmly.

I did not hear her the second time, so I look for her eyes.

When our eyes meet I hear her say, "I'm sorry."

Then she leaves the bus quickly.

Not once looking back, not once waiting for my response.

Light can murder in excess[22]

Consider the Method

1. Separate *them* from love.

Milk pours over a ledge, plopping onto the floor in decisive splats.

Some milk reverberates from the splash with the ground into the wood grain, staining its pores, while others tried to make their escape.

Imagine its streaming rush in the air in slow motion, the plummeting thin white drops isolated and gracefully diving into the kitchen tiles cream yellow surface, flattening from their three-dimensional bodies into two-dimensional flatness, searching in a sluggish movement for a groove.

The milk drops seek to find other milk drops, faint opaque tendrils forming to join a larger milk river rushing from cabinet to stove, hoping to amass around the hum of the refrigerator.

Let's return to its wide plastic body ejecting the white blood of its interior, chucking it onto the kitchen floor.

No urgent motion of hand approaches to upright it, no sense of panic at the rush of its sound, where are the humans who live in this house?

Why doesn't anyone stop its guts from spilling and making a thin milk membrane everywhere?

I'd like to draw your attention to the windowsill, to the line of black ants that have just watched their fellow ants drown in this glugging white deluge.

Their tiny black carcasses stuck in the grooves, unable to move with the tides, piling up on top of each other, blotting out the milk as if they are rising from beneath the tiles themselves, as if the kitchen was on top of an entryway to the afterlife, and the spillage of deceased bodies welled up like a geyser, a rising mound of ants so large if you glanced at it too quickly you could mistake it for a grown man quaking.

Ant-amassed tears shedding down his face, a sleek cell phone somewhere before him, a voice calling out to him from the white noise-

Light murders in excess[24]

---

24   I dream of my funeral. I stand above my cold body, hands resting on my own casket. When someone approaches to pay their respects, I try to ask them, "How did I die?" My voice floats somewhere above their ears. I am now simply knots and hair.

Light murders in excess[25]

---

25   Imagine light snowfall like cleansing,

Imagine layers upon layers of compact iced wetness.

Snow washing my body, compact compartments compartmentalized, like blinking back tears, like covering up, like purely purified.

When asked if there is a problem, I'll say quietly, "No, no, not at all."

I answer while looking down at my feet.

I want to be certain that I am still here.

Be certain that my soles still haven't yet left the earth.

My feet did not stick to the ground.

I tried willing myself past the cement into the soil, as if I could claim home by manifesting roots.

If my soles fail, I could try the veins in my neck.

Imagine these blood cells empty with oxygen, as vacant boxes.

I could fill them with roses or irises, chrysanthemums or dreams.

I could amass visions of the future.

See red like waves of petals enclosing the body in soft bruises.

I could feel bare or I could feel crimson at the cheek or my throat like a balloon too full and bursting.

A compilation of sensations that ushered me to flee rather than to stay, I could leave behind a bone or two from my body.

Or perhaps a nail bed.

Or perhaps a crown of curls.

I can't seem to land anywhere, because my feet could not stick to the Earth.

Rising, I am greeted with pressure.

Inwardly, I feel miniature, as if all my organs are small sets of kitchen-ware.

With fork-lungs and ladle-heart, I try drawing a sound soup from tongue tides.

I try singing in gasps or whispers, despite being ensnared.

I smear as a sound between rocks and fangs, and continue to rise.

The sun blinds me, while my skin cracks against the coldening atmosphere.

I imagine there is no space for me either amongst the stars, but at least I can taste briefly the thrill of flying.

Light murders in excess[26]

Light murders in excess[27]

27   Light wants to transmute the body into vacuum, edge a mouth until bottomless; stretch out the gut towards insatiable.

Light sharpens and smooths out nerve endings, files the bone into dust.

It seeks out emptiness to expand. A shape of longing, light tried to call first love, then named desire.

Light's coarse tongue scraps the void, searching and seeking the end beyond endings, a grand taste of limitlessness.

To the light, to the light, I break open like an egg over an iron skillet.

Yoke sliding across the hot oil surface, attempting to sing as sizzle like heat running down thighs, a brandishing between dream seams, a building beneath body swirling: careened knees, right arm ricocheted, the skull afloat, the neck a door, the nipple tender fruit softly bruised blue waters see glimmer, breached.

My body, now your telescope.

Fish here.

I remember my body disappeared one night replaced by sunbeams in the morning.

I am now curtain and perhaps wind.

I assume this must be how ghosts feel, so much passing through.

Like gauze, I settle along the edges of a bright light trying to hold on.

I am a threaded cord, knotted around a trunk,
but subject to the breeze.

Flailing about, upside down; toes toward the sky, waiting patiently for the sensation of blood rushing to my head.

Is there a perspective here? A sound of a pulse?

The vein at my temple, a squeezed sensation of red reds.

No luck.

I suppose I need a familiar touch to bring me back down to Earth.

But what is familiar, when everything is now strange.

My lips feel frothed, my tongue a carp, my hair a scattering of leaves.

Touch and taste splinter across sections of time.

Which hour second future lapse is here?

There is a gap in my stomach, no urge to feed, no synapse shock, no release.

Light murders in excess[2829]

---

28 When your life flashes before your eyes. Skip the everyday. Pause and only see the highlights. Like a fly hugging the static, let me become nostalgic against the screen. I am not comfortable with silence, I need the white noise to fall asleep. Erase the distinction between heartbeat and dreams. When counting sheep, count breaths. Not backwards and just exhales.

29 Three.

    Six.

        Six-

Light murders in excess[30]

---

30   teen.
Twenty-three.
       Thirty-
              five.
I lose track

Light murders in excess[31]

---

31 of time, a pain like a bulb lodged behind my eye somehow shining brightly with no photonic stream. Saliva gathers like moss. I wonder if a spider will kill itself leisurely walking down my throat. I attempt flight to dodge this unrelenting ache but fail, stumbling instead into a blank room. White ceiling. White floor. White walls. Smooth and unblemished. Is this like *The Matrix*, where everything is an illusion? I'm not a major enough character to live through the second act. At least it will be quick, our disconnect with violence necessitates the speed in which it occurs. The accumulation escalates at a rapidness one can't easily quantify. A body here, a body there. Two dozen. Three thousand. Already stilled, already soundless. Messages relayed at speeds of light. Isn't that the beauty of the stars? They're already gone. All we know of them is their shine; how they lift us from the mundane, how our bodies expand to greet them.

I am dewed exhale.

Snaking hips slinking and winding against the wind.

I am already pieces, smooth and wet; this map of flesh a whole form like peach pit.

Tongue the grooves, suck on this residue fruit meat, taste me.

There is a legible space between memybody and what can be proven.

Like chafed red and

blood red

and beet red

flush red,

shame red,

holy reds.

Tartness covers red mouth and red tongue.

Prelude to sanctify me as both temple and altar for you to pour libations onto, like reams of paper falling upon my face, my eye, my arms, my mind.

I try to hold onto my, to assert possession of my own body.

There is strawberry jam everywhere, my throat rapt, ajar, gliding, you are already inside my blood melting soft boiling heat inside my ear cum at the bank of my gums, how do I feel

tell me

tell me

tell me,

tell me.

Light murders in excess[32]

.

---

32   I realize that perhaps my body could be like glass. I raise my arms and lean from the right side of my hip into the glare. Try to allow the light to pass through me, as if no skeleton or pigment is there. I let it in, whilst letting it out. I become sensitive to the wind, aware of the metals in the air. I taste copper or is it my blood? My legs tumble away from me, a glow blooming across the eyelid. Before I became light fully, I lost color entirely.

Light murders in excess[33]

---

33   My chest broke first with the force of its saturation.

Consider the Methods

1. When building systematic structures, it is often easiest to mimic the qualities of a net.
2. A net will always already be cast out far enough to provide the illusion of freedom.
   a. Simultaneously, there will be no means of escape.
3. If the systematic structure, like the net, comes into view. Its expansive weave engenders alarm, panic, sensations of overwhelming helplessness, even nausea.
4. Over time, the net will diffuse. It will become the water itself.
   a. It is most successful when it is imperceptible, like breathing. Or like when the eye catches the light, and becomes dazzled.
      i. Alternatively, the net remains, but has become so integrated in a subject's environment that the sight of it no longer evokes alarm, but instead a sense of security. The net is now a foundation of safety, of love.

34   I glimpse an ocean of daisies, of lilies, and strings of jasmine. I try to look into the light directly, hold onto the quality of this vertigo, the color of the blotches across my retina, the feeling of air across my holes. For a few hours I float like this.

35 I try to imagine every wound as a point of possible escape.

The sun peeks out from over the hills in the east.

The sky is orange with an underbelly of pink throughout.

I only think of pollution and splendor as it painted the bay in slate gray and lavender.

My eyes become tongues, I drink in the wave lines, the smoldering smoke against stratocumulus sides, the jagged bodies of rust and salt and the thin silk of morning veils

I become only cheeks:

perhaps
rosy
perhaps
flat
perhaps
soft
perhaps
tender

In that distance between morning in the west and the sun as it reaches across the sky

---

36 I wonder if death will feel different or the same.

37 Instead of trying to fly into the mouth of the star, I attempt landing.

Arms across my chest, thighs clamped together with my feet pointed downward.

Eyes open.

Consider the Methods

1. A system works best when there is always a sensation of threat quietly hanging over a population.
   a. One might try to point it out, by turning around sharply with a finger outstretched shouting "there!", but a mirror replaces its presence.
      i. The onlookers who you might have been meaning to enlighten to the structure's presence, stand about in confusion.
      ii. The perpetrator appears to be you; your guiltiness confirmed by the shock spreading across your own visage.
         1. In your bewilderment, you act (understandably so) emotionally.
2. Systematic structures believe themselves to be supported by rational and orderly logic.
   a. Your emotional response undermines your claim.
      i. It appears after all, to the onlookers, that you, yourself are to blame.
3. The point of grievance is suddenly deferred; the point of concern becomes instead your outburst.
   a. Your outburst's disorderliness; the mere ruckus of your exhale or the peal of your sobbing or the melting waves of your rage appear outlandish, funny even.
      i. The onlookers may apply some autotune; transform the scene into a catchy, sing-along phrase.
4. Here, this attempt at exposure has been transmuted through the mouth; chewed and regurgitated as a small river of handheld

mirrors that falls onto the ground.

    a. Glass breaks and in its many reflections, you stand silently mouthing words.

    b. You are pointing to the maw above you that has been there all along. Several rows of teeth smile and open wide.

        i. The maw bends towards the space where you were standing.

        ii. Suddenly you are suddenly gone.

ACKNOWLEDGMENTS

I want to give a heaping amount of accolades and adoration to the following people.

J.K. Fowler for believing in my work and initially picking it up under Nomadic Press.

Michaela Mullin for being a wonderful editor, and honoring my vision of the work.

As Nomadic Press formally dissolved, J.K. also brought this, along with many manuscripts, to a new home. I would like to thank Black Lawrence Press and Diane Goettel for welcoming this book with open arms and bringing *Phosphene* to physical form. I am eternally grateful for this sequence of events; it's my first official book and I am so ecstatic for it to be out in the world.

I want to thank my cohort of Mills College who were the ones to see the early stages of this work and gave me much needed feedback in its formative stages.

I'm especially grateful to my mentors there: Julianna Spahr, Truong Tran, Stephanie Young, Ari Banias, and Tongo Esien Martin. You gave me your care and attention and pushed me to become a better writer where it matters.

Special shout out to Stephen Best, from UC Berkeley, who let me partake in his stunning class, ~~Black~~ Abstraction. It was a wonderful class that really invigorated my theory-loving brain while also showing me work that still inspires and moves me today.

Thank you to all my dear loves at the Patrice Lumumba Writing Workshop; you held me throughout the pandemic, while offering me a space to continue my writing practice. Without all of you, I don't know where I would be mentally right now. Thanks for giving me so much nourishment week to week while we were sheltering in place.

I'd like to thank all those who took time to write words of praise and encouragement to *Phosphene*: Sarai Bordeaux, Meilani Clay, Jzl Jmz, Melissa Jones, Clare Lilliston, and Landon Smith. I appreciate the labor and space you made for this book.

I want to give a special shoutout to my mother and my sister! I love you both dearly.

I also want to thank my friends who have kept me soft and tender over the years and who have believed and supported me throughout this journey. I love you each to pieces.

My last, but certainly not least, special shoutout is to two people who have been extremely formative to my point of view and craft: the late great alchemical wordsmith and artist, Theresa Hak Kyung Cha, and the living bountiful queer troublemaker, Alexis Pauline Gumbs. I can say so many things about both of you here, but I will keep it short. You emanate what is possible, when is possible, and the echoing song of memory, and it has healed me time and time again.

CHRISTIAN URRUTIA

BRANDON LOGANS is a poet from Oakland, California with an M.F.A in Poetry from Mills College. His work has been published in the *Patrice Lumumba Anthology, Foglifter, Variety Pack's Special Issue Black Voices of Pride*, and *Action, Spectacle*. He might describe himself as a rectangular sheet of honey 30" x 62", 6" above any surface.